*How do snow crystals form? What shapes can they take?*

*Are no two snow crystals alike?*

These questions and more are answered inside this exploration of the science of snow, featuring photos of real snow crystals in all their beautiful diversity. Perfect for reading on winter days, this book by a nature photographer and a snow scientist will inspire wonder and curiosity about the marvels of snow. Plus, for aspiring snow crystal scientists, don't miss the snow-crystal-catching instructions in the back!

★"With never a hint of hyperbole, the authors communicate such a contagious sense of wonder that few readers will be able to resist." —*Booklist,* starred review

★"The sort of riveting exhibition that will have eyes locked to the pages." —*The Bulletin of the Center for Children's Books,* starred review

"Sure to get young scientists outside." —*Kirkus Reviews*

"Libraries in areas where snow falls will definitely want to add this title to their collections, but it would enhance lessons on weather anywhere." —*School Library Journal*

"This account harnesses our everyday delight in snowflake shapes to draw us into the scientific explanations for their formation and variety." —*The Horn Book*

A Bulletin of the Center for Children's Books Blue Ribbon winner
An NSTA Outstanding Science Trade Book for Students K-12
A Chicago Public Library's Best of the Best
A Junior Library Guild selection
An American Meteorological Society Louis J. Battan Author's Award winner
An American Association for the Advancement of Science (AAAS) / Subaru SB&F Prize finalist
A New York Public Library 100 Best Titles for Reading and Sharing

National Science Teachers Association NSTA Outstanding Science Trade Book CBC Children's Book Council

*For Pam*

*—MC*

*To Yasuko for helping me with this book. From you, I learned much, and hope your efforts mean that our kids Shizuho and Asaki appreciate seeing their names mentioned here.*

*—JN*

First Chronicle Books LLC paperback edition, published in 2017.
Originally published in hardcover in 2009 by Chronicle Books LLC.



ISBN 978-1-4521-6436-6

The Library of Congress has cataloged the original edition as follows:
Cassino, Mark.
The story of snow : the science of winter's wonder / by Mark Cassino ; with Jon Nelson.
p. cm.
ISBN 978-0-8118-6866-2
1. Snowflakes. I. Nelson, Jon, Ph.D. II. Title.
QC926.32.C37 2009
511.57'84—dc22
2009004368

Manufactured in China.

Design by Annie Tsou.
Illustrations by Nora Aoyagi.
The illustrations in this book were rendered in watercolor and ink.
Simple plate image on page 17 by Fred Widall.
Typeset in Bodoni Egyptian and Neutra Text.

20 19 18 17 16 15 14 13 12 11

Chronicle Books LLC
680 Second Street
San Francisco, California 94107

Chronicle Books—we see things differently.
Become part of our community at www.chroniclekids.com.

# *The Story of Snow*

The Science of Winter's Wonder

By Mark Cassino with Jon Nelson, Ph.D.

*illustrations by Nora Aoyagi*

chronicle books · san francisco

Our story starts on a winter day,
high up in the sky,
in a cloud that is very,
very cold.

*This is the story of snow.*

*Clouds are mostly made of air, which we can't see. Then there is water vapor (water in the form of a gas), which we also can't see. We do see the billions of tiny droplets of liquid water and ice crystals that float in the cloud. They reflect light, making the cloud visible.*

## *Snow begins with a speck.*

Clouds are mostly made of air and water, but there are also bits of other things, like tiny particles of dirt, ash, and salt. Even living bacteria can float in the wind and end up in a cloud. A snow crystal needs one of these "specks" to start growing.

These specks are all much smaller than the eye can see.
But if you could see them . . .

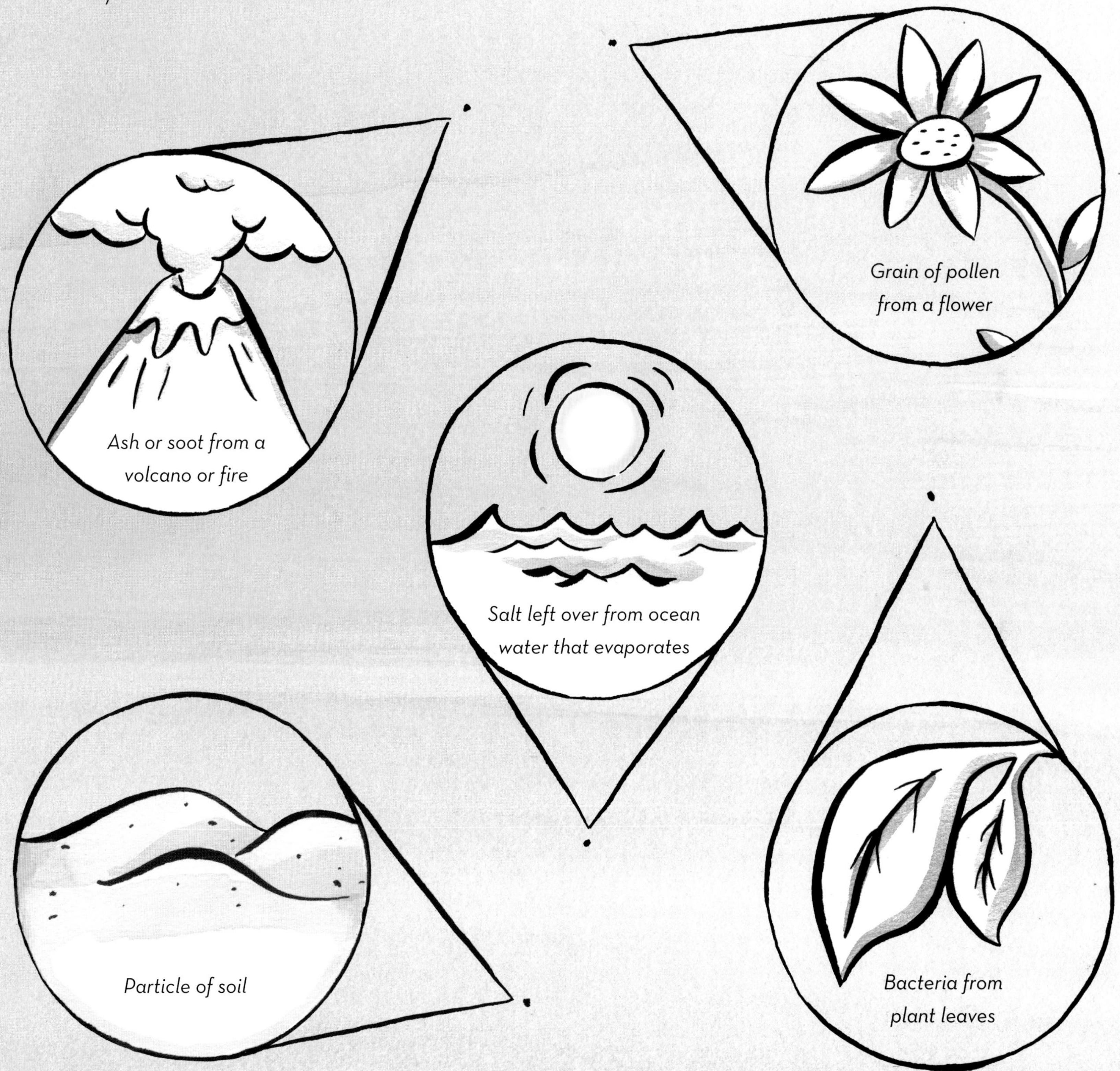

# *The speck becomes the center of a snow crystal.*

When a speck gets cold enough, water vapor will stick to it. If you had a microscope that could see such small things, here is what you would see . . .

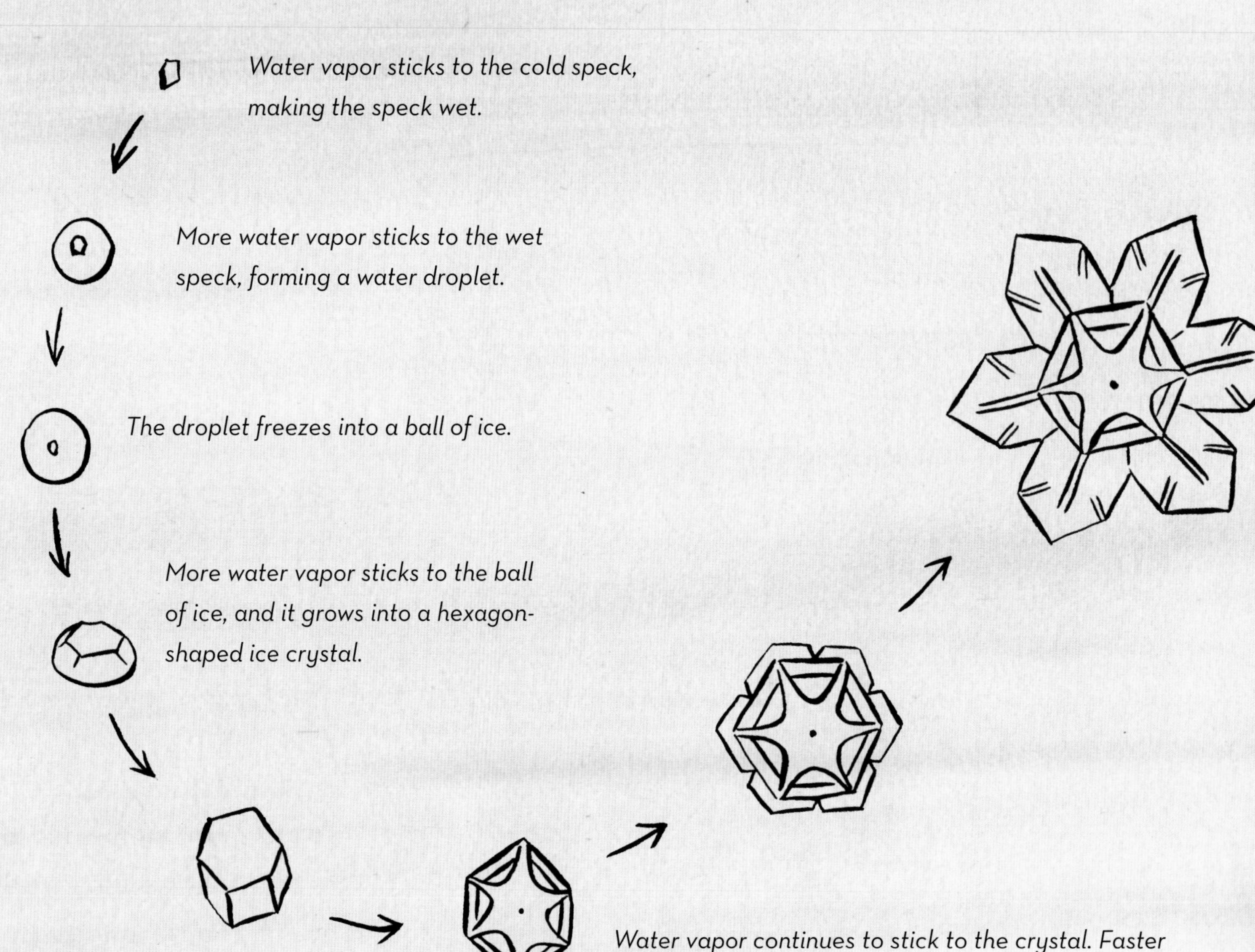

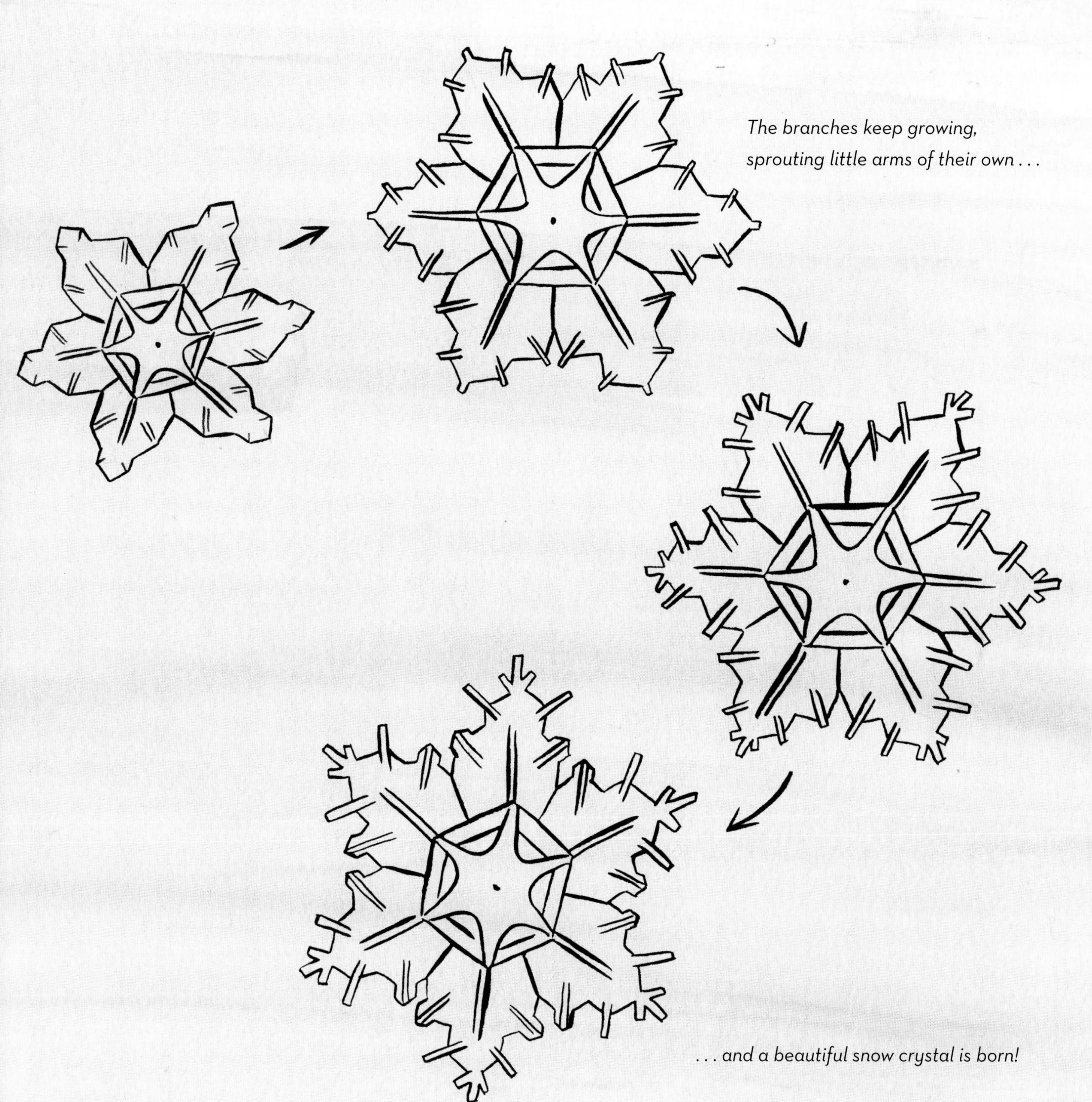

*The branches keep growing, sprouting little arms of their own . . .*

*. . . and a beautiful snow crystal is born!*

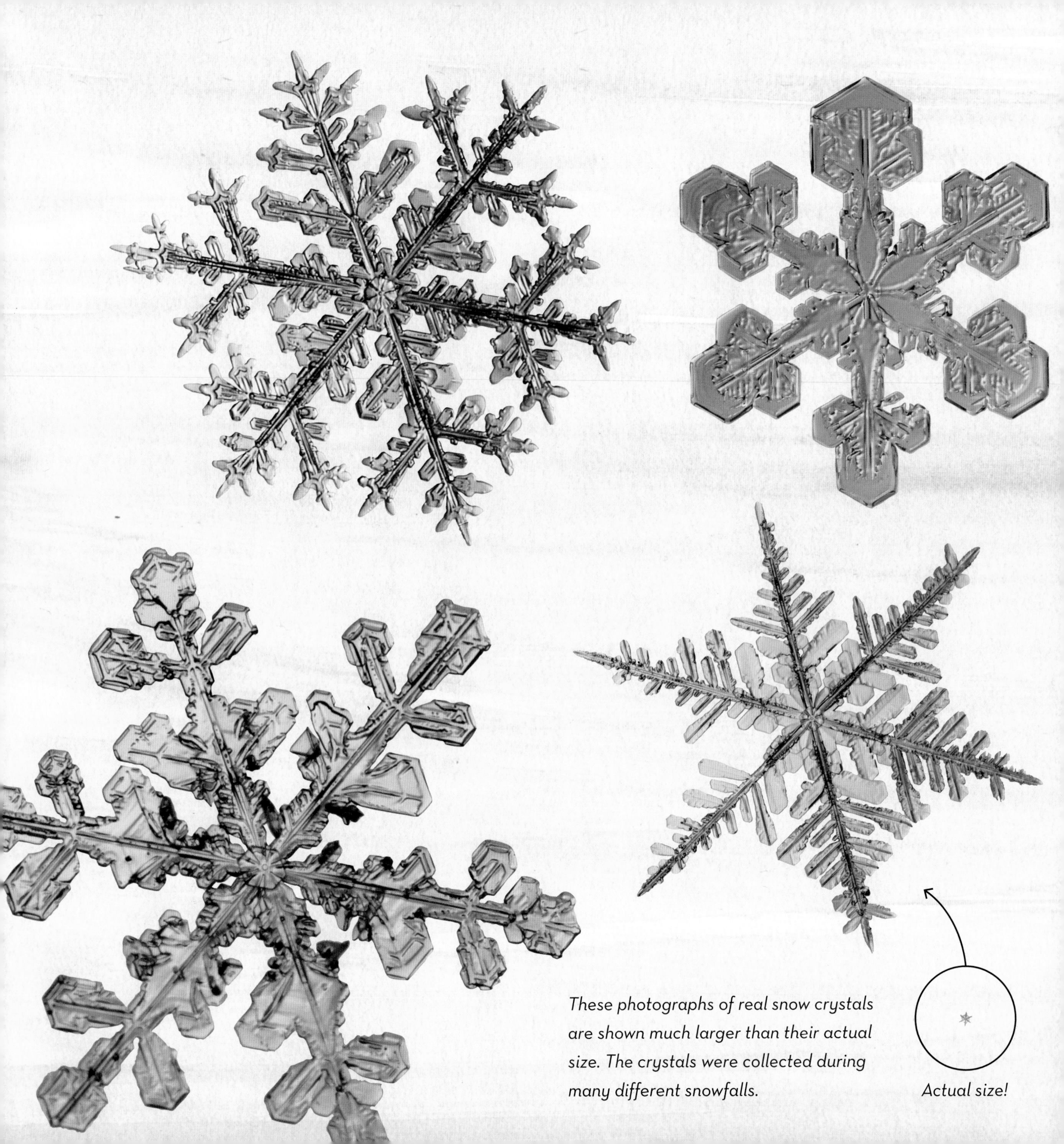


*These photographs of real snow crystals are shown much larger than their actual size. The crystals were collected during many different snowfalls.*

# *A snow crystal forms as it falls.*

As the snow crystal gets bigger and heavier, it starts to fall to earth. It keeps growing as it falls through its cloud, taking on its own special shape. The shape depends on how *wet* the cloud is and how *cold* it is. A snow crystal can start to grow one way, but then grow another way when it passes through a wetter or colder part of its cloud. The crystal stops growing soon after falling below the clouds.

*Parts of a snow crystal can break during the fall to earth, causing the arms to look different.*

# *Snow crystals can be stars.*

One common snow crystal shape is the star. Star-shaped snow crystals usually have six arms reaching out from a center point. The center point is the home of the speck that started the crystal. The six arms look alike, but they are almost never *exactly* alike.

*Star-shaped snow crystals are called dendrites (which means "tree-like"). They form when a cloud is full of moisture, and when the temperature hovers around 5 degrees Fahrenheit (–15 degrees Celsius).*

*This is the simplest kind of plate crystal, a hexagon. Plates form when there's not enough moisture in the cloud for stars to form, and when the temperature conditions are a few degrees warmer or colder than the temperature range that stars require.*

# *Snow crystals can be plates.*

Plate crystals are thin like star crystals, but they don't have arms. The simplest kind of plate is a hexagon with six straight sides. More complicated plates have points where arms almost grew.

*Simple plate crystals are much smaller than stars. They can be as wide as 1 millimeter, but they're usually a lot smaller.*

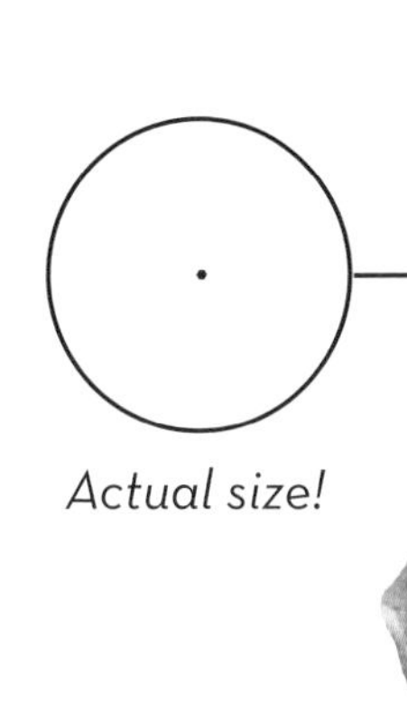

*Actual size!*

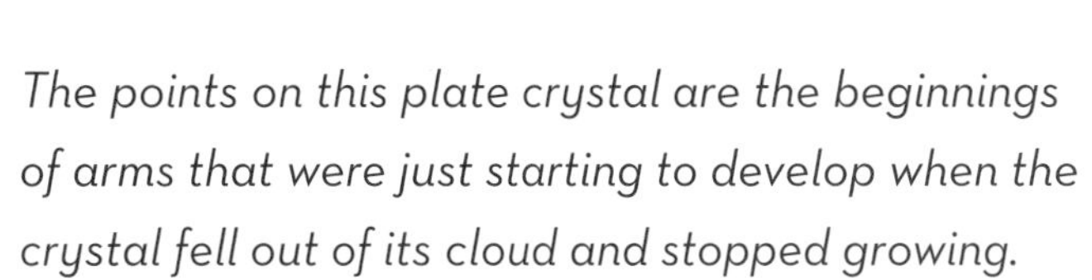

*The points on this plate crystal are the beginnings of arms that were just starting to develop when the crystal fell out of its cloud and stopped growing.*

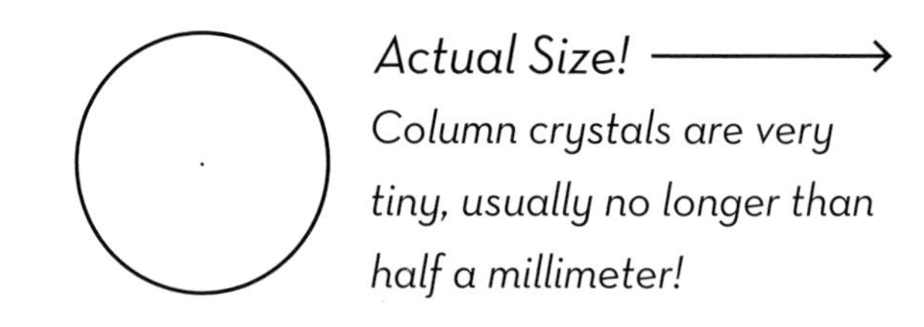


# *Snow crystals can also be columns.*

Column-shaped snow crystals are shaped like pencils. They're not flat like stars and plates. Columns can form high in the clouds and at very cold temperatures. They are *very* tiny, and when they fall, they make for very slippery snow.

*A column has six sides. These are the three types:*

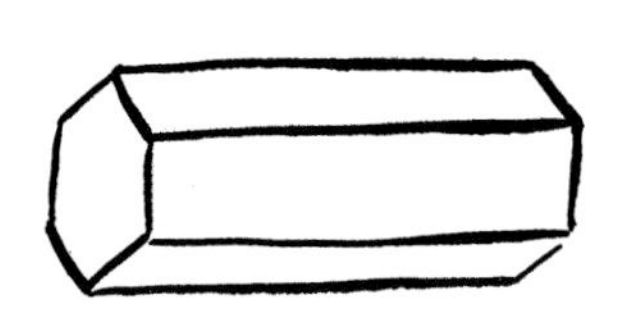

**Solid column**

*These are the smallest type of column.*

**Hollow column**

*These are longer and more common than solid columns.*

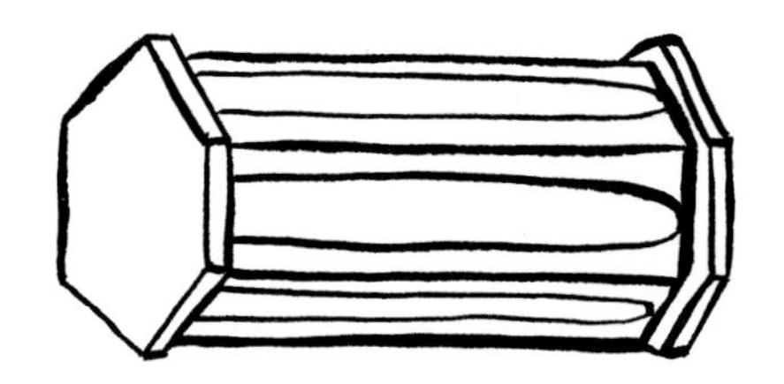

**Capped column**

*The caps on each end of these columns can be plate crystals or star crystals.*

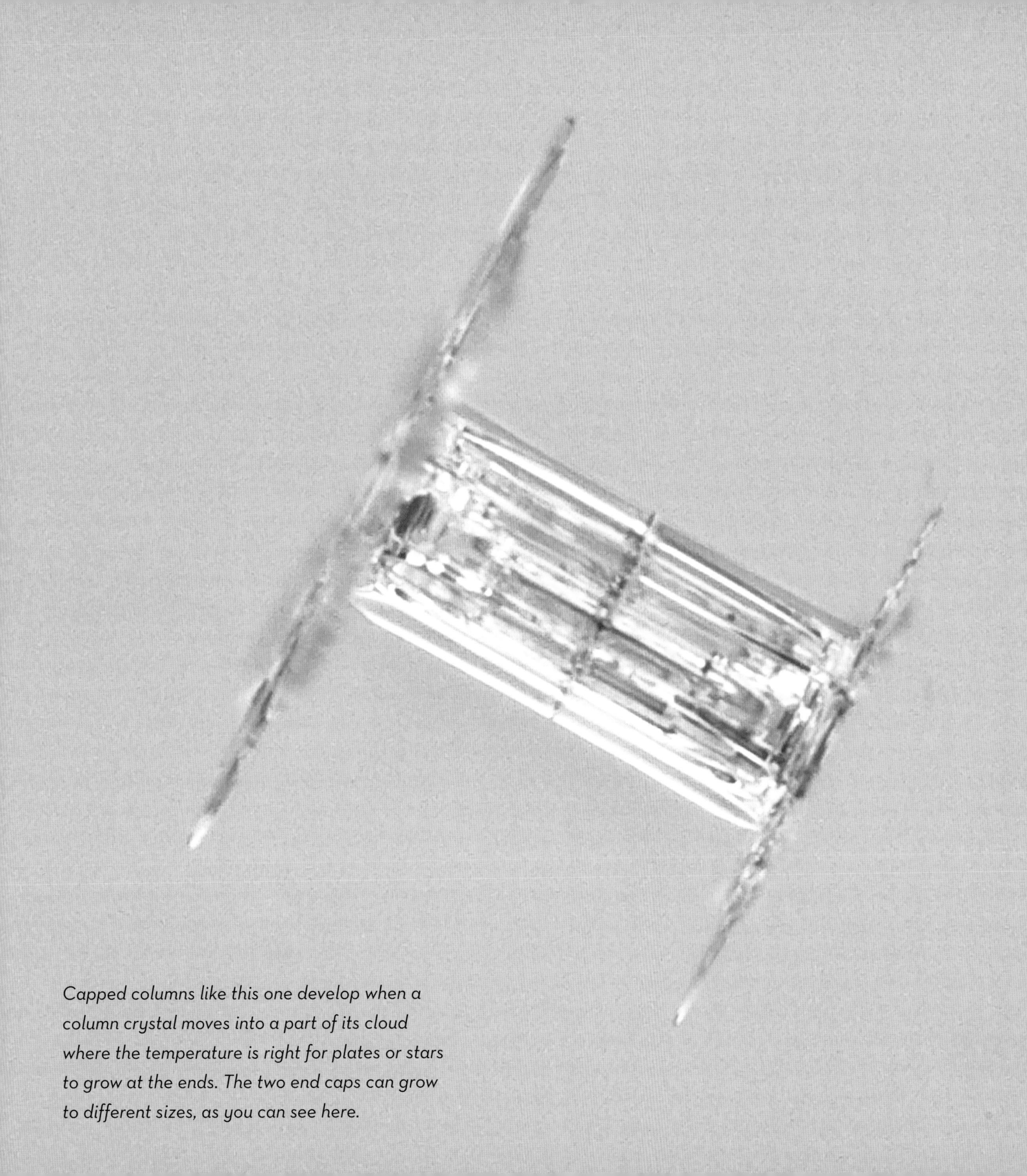

*Capped columns like this one develop when a column crystal moves into a part of its cloud where the temperature is right for plates or stars to grow at the ends. The two end caps can grow to different sizes, as you can see here.*

*If you think of a star crystal as a clock, the arms of a star crystal can point to 2, 4, 6, 8, 10, and 12 o'clock. Only those times!*

# 6 *is the magic number for snow crystals.*

This is because of the nature of water. Water molecules (the smallest units of water) attach themselves into groups of six, which usually leads to crystals with six arms or six sides.

*A perfect star or plate snow crystal has six-fold symmetry. That means, if you divided the crystal into six pie wedges, each pie wedge would have the same shape.*

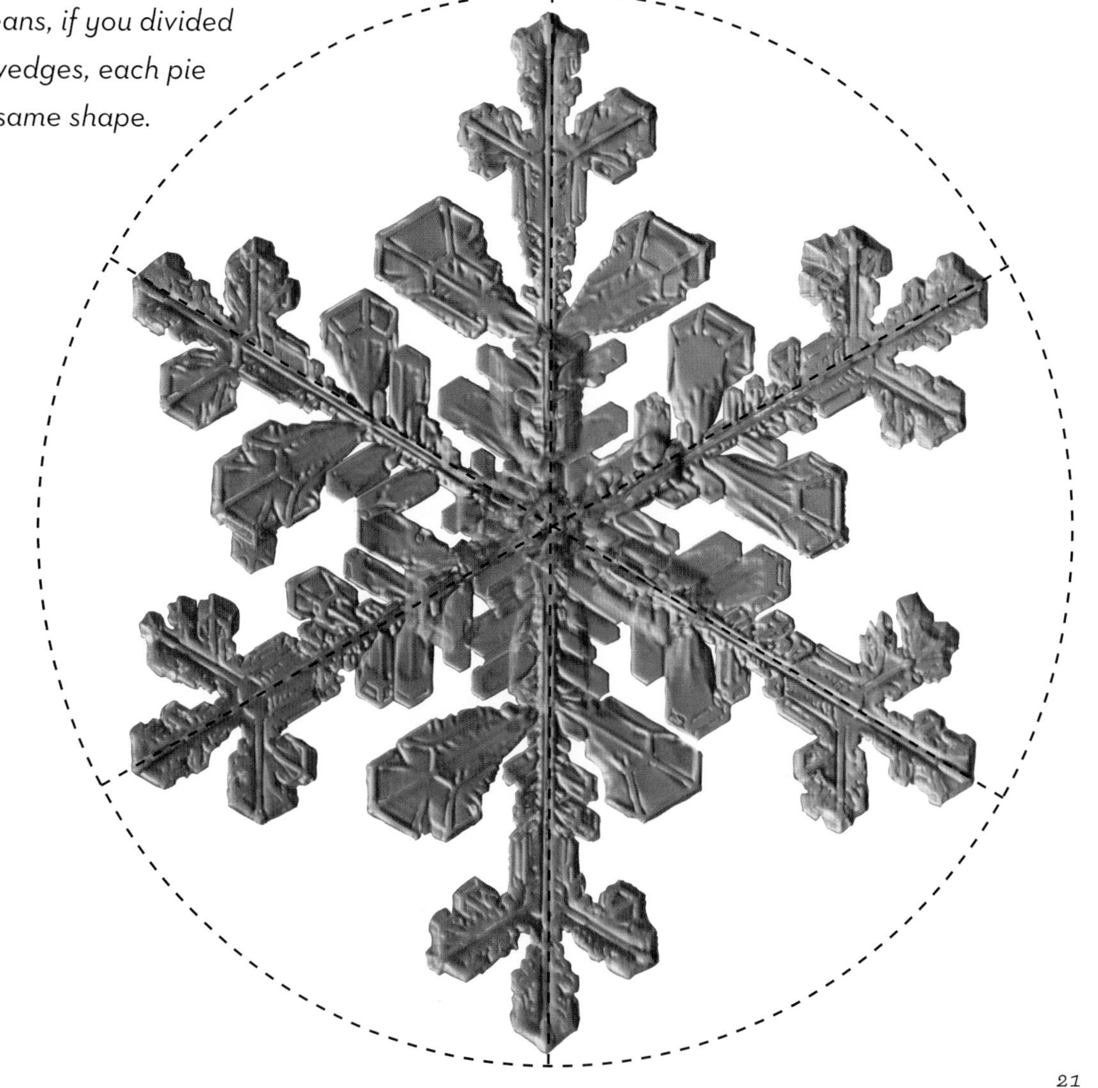

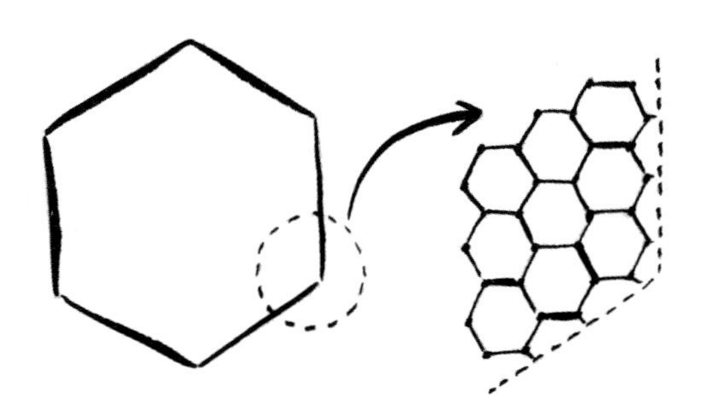

*Water molecules attach to each other in six-sided rings, like six kids holding hands. When many of these hexagonal rings are joined together, a larger hexagonal crystal is formed.*

# *Snow crystals are rarely perfect.*

So much can happen during a snow crystal's fall to earth, it is rare that one will turn out perfectly. If a droplet of water passes close to one arm of a snow crystal, that arm can start to grow faster. Before long, that one arm will be a lot longer than the others!

# *A snow crystal can be a twin!*

A snow crystal can have twelve arms. This is a twin crystal, which happens when two crystals start from the original speck and form on top of each other.

# *A snow crystal can have bumps!*

If there are enough water droplets near the crystal, some can strike the crystal and freeze on contact. This gives the crystal little bumps called rime.

# *Many snow crystals make one snowflake.*

Often, snow crystals bump into each other and get stuck together. When this happens, snowflakes form. Hundreds or even thousands of snow crystals can be found in a single snowflake.

*Two snow crystals stuck together.*

*Snowflakes we see falling from the sky are usually clumps of snow crystals like these. Individual crystals (which are sometimes also called "snowflakes") can fall on their own, but they are much smaller and harder to see.*

# *Once a snow crystal lands, it starts to wither away.*

Snow crystals can't keep growing after they fall from the clouds. And when a crystal stops growing, it immediately starts to wither. Soon, the arms of the crystal break down and the crystal's shape becomes rounded. This means that if you want to see a snow crystal, you need to catch it in the air, or find it very soon after it lands.

*When they're not in the clouds, surrounded by the water vapor they need to grow, snow crystals quickly start to erode. Try catching one on your sleeve or glove to see the crystal structure at its best.*

# *Are no two snow crystals alike?*

Some simple plate crystals may appear exactly alike, as seen through a high-quality microscope. When it comes to more complicated snow crystals though, odds are that no two are exactly alike. But then, no two leaves, flowers, or people are exactly alike, either! Snow crystals are like us—we're each different, but we have a lot in common.

# *How to Catch Your Own Snow Crystals*

## *Get Ready*

Get these things ready so you have them the next time it snows:

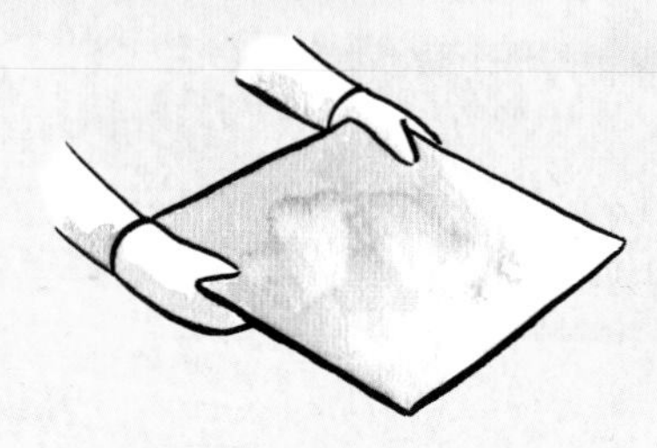

- A piece of dark cardboard or foam core board. It should be about the size of this book. Make sure that the cardboard is stiff enough to stay flat when you hold it by one edge.

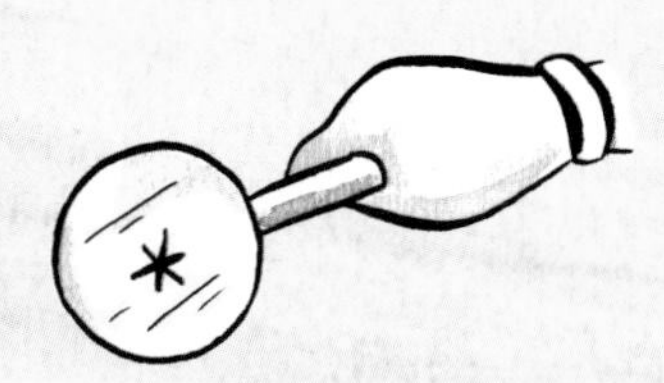

- A magnifying glass so you can see the snow crystals better.

Now . . . wait until it snows!

## *During a Snowfall*

1. Put the cardboard or foam core outside for at least ten minutes before catching snow. (It needs to be cold or else the snow will melt right after landing.) Make sure the board stays cold and dry.

2. Gripping the board by one edge, hold the board out flat and watch as the snow lands on it. If it is snowing hard, step under a porch roof or some other shelter so less snow falls on the board. Otherwise, the board will fill up with snow.

3. Look at the smaller bits of snow that land on the board. This is where you will find the individual snow crystals. Use the magnifying glass to look at them closely.

4. Once you have looked at the snow, shake off the board and try again. In the right kind of snowstorm, you should be able to see many individual snow crystals.

*Snow-Catching Tips*

- *Make sure it's cold enough! If the snow melts when it hits the board, or if rain is mixed with the snow, the temperature is probably too warm.*
- *Look for tiny snow crystals, not big snowflakes. (Remember—snowflakes are lots of snow crystals clumped together.)*
- *Sometimes the snow is all broken up and looks like a light powder. Not every snowfall has unbroken snow crystals. If the snow just isn't right, don't give up. Try again another snowy day! (Or, wait until you go on a ski trip!)*

*A snow crystal is a letter from the sky.*

*—Ukichiro Nakaya, Japanese scientist (1900–1962)*